Sadie Glover is a Partner in the family team at B P Collins LLP. She qualified as a solicitor in 2006 and practises exclusively in all aspects of family law, from the straightforward to the highly complex. Priding herself in adopting a sensitive, down-to-earth and practical approach in all cases, she draws on personal and professional experience to provide the highest level of client care.

Sadie has developed a skill for writing and delivering online training for other family lawyers across England and Wales. She recently co-presented a webinar for MBL, one of the country's leading providers of CPD training and has been retained by MBL to deliver further training on different family law topics, later this year.

In her spare time, Sadie enjoys spending time with her two daughters, Molly and Rosie and long countryside walks with their beloved dog, Phoebe. Sadie is also a keen runner and has taken part in a number of running events, to include the London Marathon.

A Practical Guide to Short Marriages for Family Lawyers

A Practical Guide to Short Marriages for Family Lawyers

Ms Sadie Glover LLB (Hons), Solicitor

Law Brief Publishing

Published 2022 by Law Brief Publishing, an imprint of Law Brief Publishing Ltd
30 The Parks
Minehead
Somerset
TA24 8BT

www.lawbriefpublishing.com

Paperback: 978-1-914608-32-2

For my girls, Molly & Rosie.

FOREWORD

Every busy practitioner knows the value of having ready access to those essential 'go to' books – the ones that will quickly give you a crucial head start when advising your client and preparing for court.

In her new book, Sadie has managed to provide a comprehensive yet accessible study charting the development of the Court's approach to short marriages from the pre-White era to the more recent authorities of *Sharp v Sharp* and *E v L*.

As an experienced barrister specialising in financial remedy cases and having known and worked with Sadie for over 15 years, I can think of nobody better qualified to author what is bound to become a defining text in this important and often nuanced area of law.

It is certainly destined to become a well-thumbed addition to my bookshelf…

Helen Jefferson, Barrister
1GC Family Law

PREFACE

First of all, thank you very much for purchasing a copy of this book. I believe that this is one of the first of its kind on the topic of short marriages and it is my first ever publication!

I was recently inspired to deliver a webinar for MBL, one of the country's leading CPD course providers, on the subject of the court's approach to short marriages. This was following my dealings with a run of short marriage cases. These cases involved many of the issues addressed in this book, from needs and sharing, to unmatched contributions. I thought that it would be useful to prepare a comprehensive guide for fellow practitioners, containing the key legal principles that have evolved in case law, from the pre-*White*[1] era, to the present day.

It should be noted from the outset for ease, references in this book will largely be made to matrimonial cases, although the same principles will apply to civil partnership cases.

I hope that you find this book useful and enjoy reading it as much as I have enjoyed writing it! The law stated here is accurate, to the best of my knowledge and belief, as at 10 May 2022.

Sadie Glover
May 2022

STOP PRESS

Just as this book was going to press, the case of ***VV v VV (2022) EWFC 21*** was reported. In this case, Mr Justice Peel considered the law on the effect of premarital cohabitation and engagement on the sharing

---

[1] *White v White (2000) UKHL 54*

principle, conduct and needs arising from a short marriage. Most of the issues raised in the case are addressed in this book, by reference to the leading case law in respect of short marriages, all of which is referred to in this recent judgement. This case does not affect the accuracy of the contents of this book, although it will undoubtedly be considered in any future editions.

ACKNOWLEDGEMENTS

I have so many people to thank for their love and support, without which I would not have been able to write this book. To my wonderful daughters, Molly and Rosie and our lovely dog Phoebe! My Mum, Wesley, Ashley and family in Somerset. My Dad, Jane and family in Coventry, I love you all. My friends, especially Trina, Siew, Sam, Piers and Amie, there are just no words! To my work family, Sue, the Partners and the family team at B P Collins, you are all absolutely amazing, I'm so privileged to work with such brilliant minds. Thank you to Tim and Garry at Law Brief Publishing for putting your faith in me with this project! Finally, to the lovely Helen Jefferson at 1GC, thank you for everything, you are just brilliant and without you, this book would not have been written.

CONTENTS

Chapter One	Short Marriages and s25 MCA 1973	1
Chapter Two	Premarital Cohabitation	9
Chapter Three	Relationship After Separation	23
Chapter Four	White and the Sharing Principle	29
Chapter Five	Miller; Needs, Compensation and Sharing	37
Chapter Six	Future Needs of the Children and the Parties	43
Chapter Seven	Short, Childless Marriages	51
Chapter Eight	Conclusion – Where Does This Leave Us?	67

CHAPTER ONE

SHORT MARRIAGES AND S25 MCA 1973

Let us start with the obvious question: What constitutes a short marriage?

While there is no standard legal definition of a short marriage, it is generally accepted that a marriage of five years or less, would be regarded by the court as short. The duration of the marriage, as we will see below, is one of the factors the court must have regard to in accordance with s25(2) Matrimonial Causes Act 1973, when determining a financial remedy case. Duration is not, of course, an isolated factor. Associated with short marriages are many other considerations, such as needs, contributions and children.

Throughout the course of this book, we will be looking at how the court treats the periods before and after the marriage, when assessing the duration of the marriage in accordance with the s25 criteria. We will also be exploring how the case law has evolved over the years and some of the key legal principles that have been established arising from these cases, that will need to be considered when it comes to advising our client. The length of the marriage will potentially have a significant impact on the claims of the parties arising from divorce. A claim arising after a long marriage will usually be far greater than one arising after a marriage of one or two years. On first blush, it might be fair to assume that a financial settlement following a short marriage would be arrived at more easily than following a marriage of longer duration, given that there is less likely to be children of the family and the marital acquest more limited. But is this in fact, a realistic assumption? We will look at how the court treats non- matrimonial property in short marriages, and how the sharing principle is generally applied in these cases. We will also consider some of the case law that has evolved since ***C v C (1997)***[1] in respect of the quantum and term of periodical payments, to the more recent case of ***FF v KF (2017)***[2] in which Mostyn J has given some definitive guidance in respect of income needs.

As we know, the length of the marriage is just one of the various factors that must be taken into account by the court as part of the s25 exercise. Over the years, the family courts have developed three key principles and extra-statutory factors in respect of financial remedy proceedings, namely: needs, sharing and compensation. In the House of Lords' decision in the conjoined cases of ***Miller v Miller; McFarlane v McFarlane (2006)***[3] these three factors were identified. As we progress through the chapters in this book, we will look at how these established legal principles should be applied in marriages that may only be a few years in duration, and whether they should apply in the same way as to a long marriage. We will also look at the position when there are children of the marriage and how the court might approach the future needs of both the parties and the children in the context of a short marriage case.

Section 25 MCA 1973

The touchstone of every financial remedy case is s25 (2) of the Matrimonial Causes Act 1973, the so called 's25 criteria'. Equivalent provision is set out in Schedule 5 Part 5 to the Civil Partnership Act 2004 at paragraph 21 (2).

---

[1] *C v C (1997) 2 FLR 26*

[2] *FF v KF (2017) EWHC 1093 (fam). (2017) All ER D 94*

[3] *Miller v Miller; McFarlane v McFarlane (2006) UKHL 24*

The power of the court to make financial orders arising from a divorce is derived from the provisions of Part II of the Matrimonial Causes Act 1973. The court has the power to make any or all of the following orders:

- Periodical payments
- Secured periodical payments
- Lump sum
- Property adjustment
- Variation of settlement
- Pension sharing

In exercising its powers, the court must have regard to "all the circumstances of the case", as well as to a list of specifically identified matters. Of course, the first consideration must be given to the welfare of any children, but thereafter to the matters set out in s25(2)(a) – (h) MCA 1973.

The s25 factors are not formulaic and not listed in any order of importance. They are simply a list of relevant considerations the court must refer to when deciding a case. They can be summarised as comprising:

- The resources available to both parties, extant and/or reasonably foreseeable;
- The financial needs of the parties, bearing in mind their standard of living, their ages and the length of the marriage, and any disabilities.

In addition to the above, the court must have regard to:

- The contributions of each party
- The conduct of each party
- Any benefit either part will lose as a result of the divorce.

S 25(2)(d) Age of the parties and duration of the marriage

As noted above, s25(2)(d) MCA 1973 directs the court to have regard to "the age of each party to the marriage and the duration of the marriage". Aside from the consideration as to why those two limbs are linked together in the same sub-section, the statute is clear in its wording. We must look at the actual "length of the marriage".

Of course, the focus of this book will be on s25 (2) (d) in respect of the duration of the marriage, however it is worth briefly mentioning the preceding reference to the age of the parties. This limb of the statute mainly goes to the issue of earning capacity and pension sharing. Clearly, a distinction could be drawn between a wife in her fifties who has never worked, with a young wife in her thirties with her whole career ahead of her. The younger wife will usually be seen to have some degree of earning capacity, whereas the older wife may have difficulty in entering the job market, following financial dependence on her spouse as the main earner, for example. Furthermore, the older woman will clearly have fewer years during which to amass savings with which to support herself in retirement. Another consideration might be, for example, that a 25-year term mortgage may not be available to the older wife and as such, the mortgage repayments would be more expensive over a shorter term. The older woman having a more vulnerable earning capacity could mean that a clean break is not possible. Finally, often with age, comes health concerns. By way of example, in ***Fields v Fields***[4] the husband was 59, worked a 70-hour week, six days per week, with a "*great deal of punishing travel*" and suffered from health conditions that were said to be exacerbated by the high demands of his professional life. The court found that this would inevitably affect his ability to work in due course. Holman J concluded that he could not "*reasonably expect or assume that the husband should continue to work as he does for much longer and certainly not past the age of about 65*"[5] Age can also be relevant to the term during which a capitalisation of income needs could be calculated. This gives rise to the so-called ***Duxbury***[6] paradox, that a young wife following a short marriage would need more significant financial provision by way of an income fund, than an older and often longer married wife, solely because she is likely to live longer.

In reality, the application of the s25 factors could lead different judges on the same set of facts to various different conclusions, all of which could fall well within the scope of their vast judicial discretion. A number of significant decided cases has established a usual approach to the as to the way in which a court will deal with a given set of facts. Prior to the landmark case of ***White***[7], the norm was than an applicant spouse would merely have their reasonable requirements met. "Reasonable requirements" was a gloss on the term 'needs of the parties' in s25(2)(b) MCA 1973, expanded to reflect that needs is a fluid concept, having regard to the other factors the court is bound to consider, such as standard of living.

---

[4] *Fields v Fields (2015) EWHC 1670 (Fam) (2016) 1 FLR 1186*

[5] Paragraph 221

[6] *Duxbury v Duxbury (1987) 1 FLR 7*

[7] *White v White (2000) HL 54*

After marriages of very short duration, the court may order no financial award at all. In the case of ***Krystman***, the marriage lasted for about two weeks and a small amount was ordered to enable the wife to adjust.

Krystman v Krystman (1973)[8]

The facts

In this case, the husband was a soldier stationed in Italy. The wife was an Italian national. The parties had an affair, which culminated in a 'shotgun' wedding in 1946, when the wife believed that she had fallen pregnant. The parties cohabited for two weeks after the marriage, before the husband was repatriated to the UK. The wife remained in Italy and their anticipated child was not born. The parties remained in communication for a short period of time, but never lived together again. Neither party supported the other financially, or sought support from the other. The husband moved in with a new partner in 1948. He obtained decree nisi in England on the basis of five years' separation in January 1972. The wife applied for financial remedy. Decree absolute was granted in July 1972. The husband and wife had similar incomes, with the husband supporting himself and his new wife on £1,300 pa, and the wife supporting herself on £1,500 pa. At first instance, the Judge ordered the husband to pay the wife £75 pa on a joint lives' basis.

The husband appealed. The appeal was allowed, and the wife's application was dismissed. In all of the circumstances, given that there was a mere fortnight of cohabitation, no children, a 26-year separation and no attempt by either party to make any contact, the court found that the husband should not be required to make any financial

[8] 3 ALL ER 247, (1973) 1 WLR 927

provision for the wife. Even a nominal order would not be appropriate, as if the husband came into wealth unexpectedly, it would not be fair for the wife to have any share in it. The case fell under the ambit of s.6(2)(a) Divorce Reform Act 1969.

Summary

- There is no standard definition of a short marriage, but a marriage of 5 years or less would usually be regarded as short.
- The duration of the marriage is only one of the many factors the court must have regard to when undertaking the s25 exercise. There is no priority in respect of the application of the s25 criteria.
- *Pre-White* case law in respect of short marriages is no longer good authority and the old 'norm' in respect of only "reasonable requirements" being met is now well behind us.
- The case of ***Krystman*** is confined to its facts and demonstrative only of what the position once was.
- It is clear that case law continues to emphasise the vast width of discretion the court has in applying the s25 factors to a given set of facts. As circumstances vary so significantly from case to case, it can be difficult to discern clear and consistent principles in this area of law.

CHAPTER TWO

PREMARITAL COHABITATION

Over the last four decades, case law has firmly established that any premarital cohabitation will be added to the length of the marriage when the court assesses the duration of the marriage. The question of premarital cohabitation first arose in ***Kokosinski v Kokosinski*** *(*1979)[9]

The facts

In 1933, a Pole (H) married a Polish woman (W) and in April 1939 a son was born to them (X). After the German invasion of Poland in 1939, H fled to England where he subsequently met an English woman (Y) in 1943. H and Y worked in a factory together until 1949, when H left to start an engineering business. In 1949, H and Y began cohabiting and Y contributed her earnings towards the upkeep of their home. In 1950, H and Y had a son, C. They subsequently purchased a family home in Kilburn in H's sole name and at around the same time, Y started working full time in the husband's business. Y's wages continued to be paid towards the maintenance of the home. In or around 1955, Y changed her surname to that of H by deed poll. In 1957, H purchased a bungalow in Wokingham, as a second home to be utilised by the family at weekends. The bungalow was purchased using money contributed by Y but was nevertheless registered in H's sole name. In 1959, he transferred one share in his company to Y, retaining the remaining 4,999 for himself. Later, he transferred 2,499 of them to C.

---

[9] *Kokosinki v Kokosinski (1980) ALL ER 1106*

In 1969 H was divorced by W (his wife in Poland). In 1971, he then married Y in accordance with the promise he had given her that he would do so upon divorcing his wife in Poland. In 1972, a new family home was purchased in Cricklewood with H's or the company's funds. Y and C moved into it, but H refused to join them. Cohabitation between H \and Y therefore ceased and was never resumed. H had over the years been sending significant sums of money to W in Poland for the benefit of W and their son, X. X visited England regularly and during his visits, also worked for H's company. In 1975 H made a Will, leaving everything to Y. Relations between W and C on the one hand and between H and W, on the other, were deteriorating significantly, and in 1976 W and C presented a petition for the winding up of the company. H subsequently agreed to sell his shares in the company to W and C for the sum of £40,000. The money was paid by c on 1 July 1977. A week later W filed a divorce petition and decree nisi was granted on the basis of H's desertion. In 1979 the property in Cricklewood where W had been living was sold for £42,000 and the loan was repaid. W thereupon had to move into a single room in the bungalow in Wokingham which was at that time being occupied by her Mother and Sister. Shortly afterwards, her shares in the company were transferred to C under a deed of trust executed by her at the time of their purchase.

In 1979 W was 56 years old and still working for the company, from which she received a gross income of £5,700 per annum. She had the use of a company car and commuted from Wokingham to the factory five or six days per week. In addition to which she had assets worth around £14,000. H continued to live in the property in Kilburn and, although he offered to pay rent to C, C felt that he had a moral obligation to house his father. H was 69 years old and had capital assets of £47,500 and an income of between £3000 and £5000 per year.

A decree absolute had not yet been granted and W applied to the court a) for an order under s 15(1) Inheritance (Provision for Family and

Dependants) Act 1975 and b) for an order under s23 (1) Matrimonial Causes Act 1973 that H should make a lump sum payment to her of £13,500 in order that she could purchase a flat nearer to her work. H argued that it would be inappropriate for the court to make a lump sum order because the court was bound by s 25(1) (d) of MCA 1973 to have regard to the duration of the marriage and the marriage had in fact only subsisted for a few months. Further, the court was bound by s25(1) (f) to have regard to W's 'contribution to the welfare of the family' only during the subsistence of the marriage and could not take into account her contributions during the 25 years that H and W were cohabiting prior to their marriage.

The court found that the use of the phrase "duration of the marriage" in s25(2) (d) showed that the period between the ceremony of marriage and the final break up of cohabitation, was likely to be the most material; and:

The word "family" in s25(2)(f) referred only to events which had occurred after the ceremony of marriage. However, the court was bound by s25 (2)(f) to have regard to both the contributions of the parties and all the circumstances of the case. It could take account of the wife's behaviour, which had occurred outside of the span of the marriage. It was the function of the court to reach a financial resolution for the parties, which was fair, just and reasonable. The court could not do justice between the parties unless it took into account the wife's conduct during the 25 years of cohabitation. The court found that she had been a faithful, loving and hardworking wife, and had helped to build up the family business, whilst at the same time managing the home and helping bring up the parties' son. In the circumstances, the husband's arguments failed to succeed.

We can therefore see how this case paved the way for a change in judicial thinking, about premarital cohabitation. Of course, matters evolved further, following the landmark case of ***White***[10], which will be analysed in more detail later in this book.

One of the leading cases to take note of in respect of premarital cohabitation is the case of ***GW v RW (2003)***[11].

The facts

In this case, the parties were married in April 1989. Prior to the marriage they had cohabited for around 18 months. In 1995 the wife presented a divorce petition to the court, although the same was dismissed around 18 months later when the parties reconciled. Around five years later a second petition was issued by the wife and a decree nisi was granted in December 2001. The parties had significant assets which were largely amassed from the husband's employment. The wife issued ancillary relief proceedings seeking an equal division of the capital assets. It transpired in the course of the proceedings that the husband had made errors on his Form E, with the effect that there was a huge discrepancy between the parties' respective computation of the assets. The parties had made a number of ***Calderbank***[12] offers, the husband's being around 40% and the wife's 50% of the assets.

The court found that it would be unfair not to include the period of cohabitation preceding the marriage where there had been no major change in the way in which the parties lived, as part of the duration of the marriage. Further, it would not be right to include in that definition a period where there had been a formal and defined separation. Therefore, the duration of the marriage in this case was determined to be one of just over 12 years in total. At that time, an

---

10 *White v White (2000) UKHL 54*

11 *GW v RW (2003) 2 FLR 108*

12 *Calderbank v Calderbank (1975) 3 ALL ER 333*

assumption of equal value of contribution was obvious for marriages of over 20 years in duration, however it would be unfair for a party who had made contributions during a marriage of 12 years to be awarded the same proportion of the assets as a party who had made similar contributions for 20 years. The husband had brought an established and lucrative career to the marriage that was unmatched by the wife. Nevertheless, the court found that the parties had equal needs in terms of property and an income. The wife had no earning capacity and as such her income would have to be amortised, calculated on a *Duxbury*[13] basis, utilising a net rate return of 3.75% as recommended by the Duxbury Working Party. The husband had a substantial earning capacity and therefore, he needed no more than the wife to meet his needs. On the basis of the calculation, each party needed about 26% of the assets. In all of the circumstances, there would be a departure from equality in respect of the surplus. The wife was therefore awarded 40% of the total assets.

Following the significant judgement in this case, it is now usual for any period of premarital cohabitation to be added to the length of the marriage. The principle established following this case, is that the commencement of cohabitation in a settled relationship may be treated as the appropriate start date. This approach also reflects changes in social habits, in that now many people choose to live together prior to marriage or civil partnership.

This principle was further compounded in ***CO v CO (2004)***[14] in which pre marriage cohabitation of 8 years (followed by a four-year marriage) was given full weight where it '*seamlessly and immediately pre-dated the marriage*'. Coleridge J said that cohabitation before marriage cannot be ignored in assessing "*all of the other circumstances of the case*" as per s25(1) MCA 1973, and in seeking to achieve fairness

---

13 *Duxbury v Duxbury (1987) CA 1987*

14 *CO v CO (2004) EWHC 287*

between the parties. Therefore, assets accrued during premarital cohabitation would in some cases be treated as matrimonial.

In ***M v M (2004)***[15] Baron J said that a distinction between committed periods of cohabitation and trial periods may not be possible in all cases. At paragraph 55.5 of her judgement, she said:

> *"The relationship to which I shall have regard lasted 16 years – I do not draw any distinction between the years of co-habitation and those of the marriage in this case. I take fully into account the precise wording of the statute, but I am clear that in modern society it is a couple's commitment to each other by co-habiting that is the relevant start date for consideration in most cases. Indeed, I consider that it is the norm for most couples to live together for a period before marriage. In this case, the parties are Catholic by religion but even they did not consider their religious tenets to be any impediment to a life together without the formality of marriage. That was, as I find, because they assumed that marriage was inevitable. I am well aware of the decision in* ***Foley - v - Foley 1981 3 WLR 284*** *and the dicta of Eveleigh LJ at page 290. There are many other old cases dealing with the importance of the married years per se but I consider that society has moved on and it would be old-fashioned (indeed, senseless) to ignore the manner in which people now choose to order their lives. I prefer the modern view and draw a measure of comfort from* ***GW - v- RW [2003] 2 FLR 108*** *in which Mr Mostyn Q.C (sitting as Deputy High Court Judge) rightly said:-*
>
> *"[Foley].... is now nearly 22 years old. The case of White v White has emphasised that the law in this area is not moribund but must move to reflect changing social values. I*

[15] *M v M (2004) EWHC 688 (Fam) (2004) All ER D 83*

> *cannot imagine anyone nowadays seriously stigmatising pre-marital cohabitation as 'living in sin' or lacking the quality of emotional commitment assumed in marriage. Thus, in my judgment, where a relationship moves seamlessly from cohabitation to marriage without any major alteration in the way the couple live, it is unreal and artificial to treat the periods differently. On the other hand, if it is found that the pre-marital cohabitation was on the basis of a trial period to see if there was any basis for later marriage then I would be of the view that it would not be right to include it as part of the 'duration of the marriage'. This was the finding made in the recent case of F v F (unreported) 14 January 2003 by Hartmann J in the High Court of Hong Kong, which decision contains some valuable insights on this and other aspects of the law of ancillary relief. There is no basis for such a finding in this case, and I therefore include the 18 months of pre-marital cohabitation here as part of the 'duration of the marriage'*

She went on to say at paragraph 55.6." *In fact, I doubt that the nice distinction which Mr Mostyn sought to draw will be capable of identification in most cases. He added (at Paragraph 40)*

> *"I do not shrink from saying that this is a difficult issue. The logic deployed by Mr. Pointer has obvious force. But on the other hand it seems to me that to adopt it requires me to put a blue pencil straight through the statutory criterion of the duration of the marriage. The failure of the judge in L v L (Financial Provision: Contributions) [2002] 1 FLR 642 (Lambert) to give sufficient weight to this factor was specifically criticised by the Court of Appeal. It seems to me that the assumption of equal value of contribution is very obvious where the marriage is over 20 years. For shorter periods the assumption seems to me to be more problematic. I am not attracted to a formulaic solution, as suggested by John*

> *Eekelaar, but I do in essence accept his proposition that the entitlement to an equal division must reflect not only the parties' respective contributions but also an accrual over time".*

The case of ***Lawrence v Gallagher (2012)***[16] further highlights this principle in the context of civil partnerships.

The facts

This was a case where the parties had cohabited for 11 years prior to entering into their civil partnership, which subsequently broke down 7 months later. The claimant was an actor and the defendant an equity analyst. They entered into a civil partnership in 2007 and separated in September 2008. The claimant petitioned for dissolution in January 2009. As stated by Lord Justice Thorpe in his leading judgement, it was common ground that the civil partnership should be treated as having lasted for 11 years and seven months. Both parties owned properties and over time, the defendants flat in London which he had owned prior to the relationship became worth twice as much as the cottage which had been bought in part with the proceeds from the sale of the claimant's previous property and which was held on trust between them. The claimant sought 45% of the assets. The defendant argued that the sharing approach was not appropriate, since his flat was not a partnership asset and that the relationship should be regarded as a 'dual career relationship'.

The Judge broadly accepted the claimant's case, finding that the flat had been partnership property and had increased from £500,000 to £2.4m and found that there was no evidence to support a dual career characterisation. The total assets available for division was £4,175,000. The judge awarded the claimant £1,690,000 which

[16] *Lawrence v Gallagher (2012) EWCA Civ 394 (2012) 2 FLR 643*

included the cottage, worth £822,000, a share of the defendant's pension of £200,000 and a lump sum payment of £577,778. The defendant appealed.

The defendant argued that the judge had inter alia a) erred in not accepting the defendant's evidence that at the start of cohabitation, the flat had a value of £650,000, b) misunderstood the defendant's evidence as to his income, confusing gross with net, to his detriment and c) misunderstood his bonus scheme, incorrectly describing the deferred shares as vested and earned during the partnership. The defendant argued that the flat was a pre-acquired asset that should not be subject to the sharing principle. The claimant submitted that this was a classic case for equal sharing, with only a small discount to reflect the defendant's greater financial contribution. Consideration was given to s5 of the Civil Partnership Act 2004.

The appeal was allowed. The judge took the view that the parties had enjoyed the use of two properties during the course of the partnership. After their separation, it was evident that the defendant should have the flat which he needed for his work and the claimant the cottage. Secondly, it was necessary to consider what funds were needed for each party to live comfortably in their own homes. The defendant was self-sufficient, with earnings of just over £200,000 per year whereas the claimant's position was considerably weaker than that of the defendant. A pension sharing order was inevitable. The sources of income available to the parties would not be sufficient to redress the disparity in the value of their respective homes and the claimant's entitlement to enjoy a comfortable standard of living without suffering with financial concerns. The judge had awarded the claimant a lump sum of £577,778. That had been the sum required to bring his claim to £1.6m following the transfer of the cottage. The court of appeal found that the correct approach should have been to assess the fair lump sum based on the defendant retaining the cottage and his pension share and his pension share as the foundation for the award. Whether approached on a needs or sharing basis, a lump sum of

£350,000 was arrived at. The annual bonuses which were deferred and conditional upon performance were not capital assets but part of the defendant's income stream. There was no basis upon which the claimant should have been awarded 45% of these. That element of the judge's award would thus be removed.

In the more recent case of ***IX v IY (2018)***[17], Williams J considered the approach adopted in ***GW v RW***, (as well as other authorities), and he concluded that premarital cohabitation should be treated as either extending the period of the marriage to create a marriage of longer duration, or, as a circumstance of the case, to be taken into account in a more general way. Additionally, that cohabitation prior to marriage is relevant, because it may indicate that the parties had at that point entered into a partnership, that may be indistinguishable from those which arise after marriage.

He found that the court should be looking for "markers" as to the time which the relationship acquired "*sufficient mutuality of commitment to equate to marriage*", such as cohabitation, together with the purchase of a property, for example.

> "*In situations such as this, the court must look to an accumulation of markers of marriage which eventually will take the relationship over the threshold into a quasi-marital relationship which may then either be added to the marriage to establish a longer marriage or which becomes a weightier factor as one of the circumstances of the case.*" [para 68]

On the facts of this case, Williams J concluded that '*it is clear that the premarital relationship was, notwithstanding some ups and downs, a committed relationship, which was moving towards marriage, in which children were contemplated and hoped for and in which the pattern of life*

[17] *IX v IY (2018) EWHC 3053 (Fam) (2019) 2 FLR 449*

which developed… continued largely without change, after the marriage took place'.

This decision was considered by Cohen J in ***MB v EB***[18], which we will look at in more detail in chapter 3, who said that that analysis could be applied to *'an attempt to define the date of the end of the marriage as much to its commencement'* and that 'it *is a truism that marriage comes in all different shapes and sizes. What may be important to one couple, may be trivial to another'.*

Also see:

- ***J v J (2004)***[19] in which the date of engagement of the parties was taken into account.

- ***N v F***[20] in which while there had been a period of premarital cohabitation, there was a nine- month period of separation and the breaking off of the parties' engagement. On this basis Mostyn J said he was satisfied that the cohabitation did not move '*seamlessly into marriage and did not 'extend the span of marriage de facto by reference to the premarital relationship'.*

- ***Miller & McFarlane*** in which Baroness Hale that a determination of the duration of the marriage for the purposes of considering the extent of the matrimonial assets and duration of the marriage *"should probably include periods of premarital cohabitation and engagement".*[21]

---

[18] *MB v EB (2019) EWHC 1649*

[19] *J v J (2004) EWHC 53 (Fam) All ER D 141*

[20] *N v F (2011) EWHC 586 (Fam) (2011) 2 FLR 533*

[21] *Para 149*

- ***McCartney v Mills- McCartney*** in which Bennet J found that while the parties had a close relationship prior to the marriage, it was not *"a settled committed relationship moving seamlessly into marriage"*.[22]

In practice it can be difficult to establish a clearly defined start date of a relationship prior to marriage, although a premarital relationship may be taken into account as one of the "circumstances of the case" per Moylan J in ***C v C***[23].

> *"Parties should not be encouraged to expect the courts to enter into any extensive investigation of the nature of their premarital relationship many years later. It can also raise issues which do not appear in the Matrimonial Causes Act 1973 in specific terms and over which there could be an active debate in the search of the precise definitions."*

You may have noted that form D81 has recently been updated considerably and now specifically asks for the date of cohabitation of the parties, whereas previously it did not. The form generally is much more detailed and is designed to better assist the judge tasked with considering the fairness of the consent order and understanding the net effect of the order sought. Plainly, the length of the marriage is a key consideration in accordance both with the statute and in assessing the fairness of a proposed order.

[22] *McCartney v Mills – McCartney (2008) EWHC 401 (fam) (2008) 1 FLR 1508*

[23] *Para 62*

Summary

- It is now firmly established that the length of the marriage should be taken from the date of cohabitation through to the date of separation.

- The period may start when either cohabitation begins or at whatever point the court considers the parties became truly committed to one another.

- Premarital cohabitation may be treated as either extending the duration of the marriage, or as a circumstance of the case to be taken into account more generally.

- Premarital cohabitation is relevant when assessing whether the parties had entered into a partnership that may be indistinguishable from those which arise upon marriage.

CHAPTER THREE

RELATIONSHIP AFTER SEPARATION

It may be that although the marriage breaks down, the parties remain emotionally enmeshed with one another. If this is the case, the court might consider it inappropriate to ignore the period during which they continue to be involved. In respect of the end of a marriage or civil partnership, it is now more common for the court to look at the date of separation, rather than the date of the final decree.

Going back to ***GW v RW,*** Mostyn J said that in assessing the duration of the marriage, the court has always looked at the position *de facto rather than de jure*. For example, the end of the marriage is always taken as the date of separation, rather than the date of the decree absolute. He also took the view that it would be unrealistic to say that where the parties are estranged, with the irretrievable breakdown of the marriage being evidenced by divorce proceedings, the court could not properly count that period as part of the duration.

The date of separation was of significance in ***WG v HG (2018)***[24]. This is not a short marriage case, but it contains some interesting judgement from Francis J on how the court should treat post marriage separation.

[24] *WG v HG (2018) EWFC 84 (2018) All ER D 213*

The facts

This was a case where the wife had suffered a catastrophic brain injury following a horse-riding accident. She had made a good recovery, but had ongoing needs arising from the accident. It was the husband's position that the parties had separated prior to the accident. The wife's position was that the separation took place in the following year, albeit there had been a divorce petition presented by the husband, later withdrawn, followed by a reconciliation which the wife said was still in place at the time of the accident, and which the husband said had been quickly unsuccessful.

The practical effect of this was the question of the husband's duty to meet the wife's post- accident needs. Francis J concluded that:

> *"As a matter of pure and obvious fact, the accident occurred during the marriage, the parties were not divorced. It occurred at a time that the parties knew that the marriage was more or less over but when the wife was still completely financially dependent on the husband. The husband properly met that obligation and has continued to do so, albeit under protest"*

He added:

> *"If and insofar as the wife has a need arising from the accident, and if the husband is able to afford to meet that need, I am clear that he must do so. No one else is there to do so and there is no evidence at all that the wife would receive any state provision. I do not think in these cases it is possible to draw a line in the sand and say that if anything happens after a fixed point in time, it is nothing to do with the husband or this court. I have to make an order that is fair having regard to all of the circumstances of the case, and if I find that the wife has a financial need as a consequence of her*

> *accident, or indeed any other need, and if I find that the husband is able to meet it, then he should do so. Nor can I, in some artificial or arbitrary way, reduce the amount of support that the husband should provide to the wife, on account of the fact that the marriage was almost over at the date of the accident."*

Looking further at the way in which the court deals with the relationship after marriage, we will now consider the case of ***MB v EB (2019)***[25]. This case concerned 3 preliminary issues:

- The length of the marriage
- The extent of the marital acquest
- The impact of a 2011 separation agreement

The facts

The parties were married in 2000. The wife asserted that this was a short marriage and that the parties had separated in 2004, when they stopped living together. The husband argued that they had in fact separated in 2016, when he issued divorce proceedings.

Cohen J considered when the relationship lost "sufficient mutuality of commitment to equate to marriage"[26] and it was difficult to establish the date of separation since the parties remained emotionally enmeshed and also partly physically connected long after 2004. Cohen J found that the parties did in fact separate in 2004, since post 2004, they spent more time apart than they did together. Indeed, the husband had other relationships and a separate home from 2005 and

---

[25] *MB v EB (2019) EWHC 1649 2 FLR 299*

[26] *IX v IY (2018) EWHC 3053 (Fam) (2019) 2 FLR 449*

neither party could access the other's property. Further, they met their own income needs while apart.

Additionally, the 2011 separation agreement stated that they had separated in 2004. However, Cohen J considered it inappropriate to disregard the entire period between 2004 to 2016 from all further consideration, acknowledging that neither party had moved on emotionally until after 2016.

This was a case in which the wife's wealth emanated from her family and there was no significant marital acquest. The husband argued that vitiating factors such as duress, invalidated the 2011 separation agreement. Alternatively, that it would be unfair to hold him to the agreement since the parties did not in fact separate and holding him to it would leave him in a predicament of real need. Applying the principles in ***Radmacher***[27] Cohen J found that the agreement was valid, save that it may not meet the needs of the husband. In considering the alleged vitiating factors, Cohen J noted that it was the husband who had initiated the process leading up to the agreement being executed. The terms of the agreement also reflected the husband's own proposals. There was no evidence that the wife pressurised him or exploited her dominant position and as such, the vitiating factors were not made out.

Cohen J found that although disclosure was not mutually exchanged, the husband was aware that the wife came from a wealthy family and as such, nothing more was needed. Further, it was clear from the documentary evidence before the court that the agreement was intended to cover both the present and the future.

---

[27] *Radmacher v Granatino (2010) UKSC 42*

A reconciliation of the parties' post- divorce, may be approached in a similar way to premarital cohabitation, as was established in *S v S (1994)*[28]

The facts

The parties began living together in 1963 and subsequently married in 1969. There were two children of the family. In 1976 the wife issued divorce proceedings, which culminated in a decree absolute in 1977 followed by a consent order. The husband had been reluctant to accept that the marriage had broken down and made several attempts at reconciliation in the meantime. The husband was to remain in the family home with the children until the youngest attained the age of 18. Thereafter, the property was to be sold and the net proceeds divided equally between the parties. The husband was to pay £100 per month to the wife by way of periodical payments, but there was otherwise to be a clean break. During the Christmas period of 1977, the parties reconciled and the wife returned to the family home. The property was sold in May 1978 and a new property was purchased in the joint names of the parties. They continued to reside together until 1990 when the relationship finally broke down. In April 1992 the wife applied to set aside the consent order of 1977. In September 1992 she applied for leave to appeal out of time and sought an increase in the quantum of the periodical payments.

The court granted leave to appeal out of time and allowed the wife's appeal. The court considered that there were new circumstances which invalidated the basis upon which the order was made, as per ***Barder (1988)***[29] so that the appeal was very likely to succeed. The sale of the family home made the order meaningless and unenforceable, and the

---

[28] *S v S (Financial Provision: Cohabitation after divorce) (1994) 2 FLR 228*

[29] *Barder v Caluori (1988) AC 20*

resumption of cohabitation had undermined the other fundamental assumptions which underpinned the order. Secondly, the change in circumstances needed to have occurred within a relatively short period of time from the making of the order. That was clearly the case in relation to this particular order. The third condition to be met was that the application for leave needed to have been made promptly and although 15 years had elapsed since the making of the consent order and the parties had gone their separate ways in 1990, the wife had acted with reasonable promptness in all of the circumstances. Any original agreement had for many years been dormant with the family home having been sold in 1978. In applying the s25 criteria the court was obliged to regard the periods of cohabitation separately from the period of eight years where the parties were married. In this case the court gave considerable weight to the part the wife had played throughout the course of the relationship, including post-marital cohabitation, over circa 29 years, in being a mother to the children, running the family home and supporting the husband in his career. There was therefore to be a clean break along the ***Duxbury*** lines.

Summary

- Case law has established the principle that the date of separation is relevant to the duration of the marriage, rather than the date of the final decree.

- Post marital cohabitation is likely to be treated in the same way as premarital cohabitation.

- Each case will turn on its unique facts and the application of the s25 factors will ultimately determine the appropriate outcome of a case.

CHAPTER FOUR

WHITE AND THE SHARING PRINCIPLE

Once we have established that a marriage is short, how then do we as family lawyers go about advising our client as to how the court might approach their case? The landmark case of ***White v White***[30] obviously does not involve a short marriage however, it cannot go without a mention in this book, since it is crucial to assess the same in the context of short marriages. This case is foundational to any advice we give our clients in respect of how the court might approach their case, since the outcome of this case marked a very different approach to financial remedy cases generally, irrespective of the duration of the marriage and furthermore, the sharing principle was born.

The facts

Mr and Mrs White were married in September 1961. The wife was 26 years old and the husband almost 24. They had three children. Tragically, their eldest child was killed in the Kathmandu air crash in 1992. The remaining children were 29 and 30 respectively. The marriage broke down in 1994. A decree nisi was granted in December 1995, and this was made absolute in May 1997. Mr and Mrs White both filed applications for ancillary financial relief.

Throughout their marriage Mr and Mrs White carried on a dairy farming business in partnership. They both came from farming families. The business was successful. At the outset each of them

---

30 *White v White (2000) UKHL 54*

contributed a more or less equal amount of capital, of about £2,000. A year after their marriage they bought a farm in Somerset. Blagroves Farm comprised 160 acres of land. Blagroves itself, the property in which they made their home together, was £32,000. Of this, £21,000 was borrowed on mortgage. Mr White's father provided the parties with an interest-free loan of £11,000, together with a further £3,000 used as working capital. Over time, they bought further land, substantially increasing the size of the farm. Eventually the farm comprised 337 acres. Throughout, Blagroves Farm and all the land were held by the two of them jointly. The whole was treated as property of the farming partnership. In 1974 Mr White's father released his loan. Initially this was reflected in an increase in Mr White's partnership capital account. Ten years later Mr and Mrs White's capital accounts were merged into a single joint capital account. Blagroves Farm was the parties' principal asset, which was worth about £3.5 million.

The parties also farmed Rexton Farm as part of their partnership business. This farm also comprised over 300 acres. Rexton Farm was ten miles from Blagroves Farm, but the two were run as a single unit. Mr White's father bought this estate in 1971. He later transferred the estate into the joint names of himself and his three sons. The four of them held the estate in equal shares. In 1993 Mr White acquired Rexton Farm in his sole name. Rexton Farm was worth £1.25 million. After deduction of estimated liabilities for capital gains tax and costs of sale, the overall net worth of the parties' joint and sole assets was, in round figures, £4.6 million. At first instance the court made an award to the wife based on her needs (assessed at £980k), rather than a share in the matrimonial property. The wife subsequently appealed.

The Court of Appeal considered that the wife was entitled to a larger share of the capital, owing to her contributions to the marriage and subsequently increased her award to £1.5m. Mr Justice Holman stated that the court of first instance had taken the wrong approach, since the parties had made equal contributions during the marriage and therefore needs were not the determinative factor. Both parties then appealed.

The House of Lords allowed the wife's appeal. Lord Nicholls stressed that S25 gives no indication that financial needs should, above all else, determine the division of assets, particularly where the assets were well in excess of the parties' needs. Fairness dictates that '*there should be no bias in favour of the money-earner and against the home-maker and child-carer*'. Therefore, any surplus should not have been awarded to the husband.

In the judgement, almost four decades of jurisprudence were disregarded as discriminatory. In the process of dismissing both appeals, the House of Lords redefined the approach the court should take to the s25 exercise. The reasonable requirements approach was based upon the erroneous assumption that the party who earned the money was making a greater financial contribution than the party who undertook a domestic role and primary care of the children. S25 MCA 1973 specifically requires the court to have regard to the parties' respective contribution to the marriage, "*including any contribution by looking after the home or caring for the family*" and that these vastly different kinds of contribution should generally be regarded as equal. To do otherwise, would be discriminatory. Any award, particularly in a case in which the resources were sufficient to meet the needs of both parties, must be assessed against a "yardstick or equality". At this stage, their lordships were keen to emphasise that this did not necessarily amount to a starting point of equal division, moreover there should be a presumption of equal division of the marital acquest.

We can see from ***White*** that when dividing matrimonial property, needs [s.25(b)] are not the determinative factor in the division of assets, particularly where there are more assets than are required to meet needs. This is distinct to cases where is non -matrimonial property, irrespective of whether there is a short or long marriage. It should be noted_that this is not necessarily at odds with more modern authorities (***Sharp***[31] **and *Foster***[32]) about the division of assets in cases of short marriages, since they can usually be distinguished on the basis that the bulk of the property is non-matrimonial.

Contributions and non- matrimonial property

We will now consider how the court has approached cases where one party has contributed more than the other in a short marriage case and the principles that have been established by case law over almost two decades. Where the marriage is short, contributions are more likely to be relevant when determining what is and is not to be regarded as matrimonial property.

Foster v Foster[33]

The facts

In this case, the parties were in their early thirties, with no children and were married for four years. Both were employed throughout the course of marriage, with the wife earning more than the husband. The parties built up considerable assets during marriage, with the wife's financial contributions being significantly higher than those of the husband, largely due to her higher earnings.

The district judge sought to return each parties' contributions from before the marriage and after separation to them, whilst dividing the matrimonial property equally. This left the wife with 61% and the husband with 39% of the assets. The wife appealed on the grounds

---

[31] *Sharp v Sharp (2017) EWCA Civ 408*

[32] *Foster v Foster (2003) EWCA Civ 565*

[33] *Foster v Foster [2003] EWCA Civ 565.*

that judge did not give enough weight to her matrimonial contributions. The circuit judge allowed the wife's appeal, on the basis of her greater matrimonial contributions and increased her share to 70% and reduced the husband's share to 30%. The husband then appealed to Court of Appeal. The Court of Appeal allowed the husband's appeal and restored the order of the district judge on the grounds that:

(a) There should be no discrimination between the parties on the basis of their respective roles and that one earnt more than the other. The marriage and its financial success was a joint enterprise, which the parties ought to be able to share in equally.

(b) The fact that the marriage was a short one was irrelevant to how the wealth generated during the course of the marriage should be divided.

(c) The circuit judge could only interfere with the district judge's order on the basis of procedural irregularity or because the decision was plainly wrong. Neither applied and therefore the circuit judge was wrong to interfere with the district judge's decision at all.

This case applies ***White*** to a short marriage, indicating that s25 factors are applied equally (without any one factor predominating) when dividing the matrimonial property from a short marriage. Even in the context of ***White*** and ***Foster***, it is possible to depart from the 'yardstick of equality' where one individual made an overwhelming contribution to a short marriage. Business and financial contribution is more likely to be considered 'unmatched' in a short, childless marriage, which has not generated many needs. These cases highlighted the distinction between matrimonial and non-matrimonial property and that a short marriage may make this distinction more apparent, thereby justification for a departure from overall equality.

In the context of contributions, ***Charman v Charman (2007)***[34] remains one of the largest awards in financial remedy proceedings to this day. In this case, the wife received an award of £48 million, amounting to just under 37% of the total matrimonial assets. The judge ordered a departure from equality, notwithstanding that all of the assets were matrimonial, because he accepted the husband's "special contribution" to the marriage. "Special contribution" was a concept of which the Court of Appeal approved, suggesting that it would generally lead to an unequal division of assets, departing from equality up to a maximum of around two-thirds.

The issue of special contributions was also successfully raised in ***Cooper-Hohn v Hohn (2014)***[35] in which Roberts J recognised the husband's "financial genius" and the significant wealth he had generated as a result. The wife was awarded $530 million, which was around 36% of the parties overall personal assets.

Non – matrimonial property

The Court of Appeal in ***Charman*** confirmed that the application of the sharing principle would lead to an equal division of the marital acquest, unless there was a justifiable reason to depart from equality. Notably, the Court of Appeal also considered that the sharing principle applies to both matrimonial and non-matrimonial assets, albeit the provenance of the assets would often be a good reason to depart from equal sharing.

We will see later in the book, that in a small minority of cases, a short marriage with no children, dual career and separate finances may well justify departing from the sharing principle. Mostyn J's view was that such cases are as rare as a "*white leopard*" and that it is discriminatory

[34] *Charman v Charman EWCA Civ 503*

[35] *Coopher Hohn v Cooper Hohn (2014) EWHC 4122*

for childlessness to have any effect when applying the sharing principle."[36].

In ***WM v HM (2017)***[37] Mostyn J provided guidance in respect of applying the sharing principle. Mostyn J confirmed that the first step is to calculate the quantum of the matrimonial property and then to divide that equally between the parties, leaving the non-matrimonial property with the party who brought it into the marriage.

So, is the approach different to sharing and contributions, whether you are dealing with a short or long marriage? It would appear from the cases above that the answer is probably not. The court must always apply the s25 criteria to each case and duration of the marriage is just one of the limbs of consideration. The approach to each case must be the same, albeit that the outcome may be slightly different when dealing with a short marriage, as we will see in due course.

Summary

- Matrimonial property falls to be shared irrespective of the length of the marriage.
- There should be no discrimination between the parties on the basis of their respective roles within the marriage.
- Parties who divide their roles into homemaker and breadwinner will not necessarily be considered to have made different contributions.

---

[36] *K v L [2011]*[36] *EWCA Civ 550* and *Y v Y*[36] *[2012] EWHC 2063 (Fam)*

[37] *WM v HM [2017] EWFC 25 paragraph 11*

- The marriage and its financial success is regarded a joint enterprise, which the parties should share in equally. To do otherwise would be discriminatory.

- It is possible to depart from the principle of equality where one individual has made an overwhelming contribution to a short marriage.

- Fairness may necessitate a departure from equality where one party has made an unmatched contribution, even where there are assets surplus to needs. Determination of this principle requires a fact specific case by case analysis.

- Sharing of non-matrimonial property absent a needs based argument is extremely rare.

CHAPTER FIVE

MILLER; NEEDS, COMPENSATION AND SHARING

In the landmark conjoined cases of ***Miller v Miller; McFarlane v McFarlane (2006)***[38], the House of Lords identified three principles in respect of the making of financial orders:

- Needs (generously interpreted)
- Compensation for relationship- generated disadvantage
- Sharing of the fruits of the marriage

The main objective of the application of these principles is to achieve a fair outcome. In Baroness Hale's judgment in relation to sharing, she said that the court is expressly required to consider the duration of the marriage in accordance with s25(2)(d). In circumstances where the assets are non-matrimonial, or generated by the joint efforts of the parties, then the duration of the marriage may justify a departure from equality[39]. Lord Nicholls in his minority judgement said that to confine the White approach to the "*fruits of a long marital partnership*" would result in the discrimination White was intended to eradicate[40].

---

[38] Miller v Miller; McFarlane v McFarlane (2006) UKHL 24 (2006) 1 FR 1186

[39] Para 152

[40] Para 19

We have seen that in ***Charman***[41] the Court of Appeal confirmed that the application of the sharing principle would lead to an equal division of the fruits of the marital acquest unless there was a good reason to depart from equality.

Miller v Miller; McFarlane v McFarlane (2006)

The facts

This case involved a childless marriage lasting less than three years, where the husband was a very high earner and the wife was homemaker. The judge at first instance awarded the wife £5m, out of the husband's assets valued at circa £17m, at separation. Much of these assets had been generated during the course of the marriage. The judge eschewed the yardstick of equality, largely because he found that the assets were not generated by joint effort. The husband had used pre-matrimonial wealth and expertise to generate the bulk of the marital acquest. The husband appealed the first instance decision. The Court of Appeal upheld that award. The husband appealed again. The court found that the award was within the discretion of the judge and should stand. Per Nicholls LJ [para 17] –

> '*A short marriage is no less a partnership of equals than a long marriage. The difference is that a short marriage has been less enduring. In the nature of things this will affect the quantum of the financial fruits of the partnership.*'

The court of Appeal found that both lower courts were wrong to take account of the husband's conduct in bringing the marriage to an end (by an affair), as it fell far short of the threshold required by s.25(2)(g). Further, the judge should not have over-emphasised the legitimate expectation given by the husband to the wife that in the future she

[41] *Charman v Charman (2007) EWCA Civ 503*

would be living on a higher economic plane, which was presumably a reference to the high standard of living enjoyed by the parties during their short marriage. We can therefore see that the court cemented the general approach from ***Foster*** that ***White*** principles apply to the matrimonial property in short marriages as well as long ones.

We can discern, following ***Miller,*** that short marriage cases are now decided by the parallel application of the two principles of sharing and needs (compensation has yet to be engaged in any short marriage case). The authorities make clear that the result should be the higher of the two figures generated by the principles.

Needs

Of the three principles, only "needs" (although without reference to generous interpretation) appears in s25(2). Needs refers to the income and capital needs of the parties, however there is no standard definition in respect of the same. Case law has interpreted the meaning broadly. "Needs" will generally trump everything in a case. As such, the provenance of wealth in a needs-led case will count for little. That being said, the court will generally and where possible seek to enable a party who introduced an asset that may be non-matrimonial in nature to retain it. That sometimes will result in the other party being allocated a larger proportion of the matrimonial assets, so that needs are met on both sides. In some cases, it may be necessary for there to be an order dealing with the resources at some point in the future, by way of a ***Mesher*** order, for example[42]. This is to ensure that the needs of the spouse with whom the children mainly reside are met during the children's minority, whereafter their needs might be similar.

[42] *Mesher v Mesher (1980) All ER 126*

Compensation

In some circumstances, consideration may be given as to whether to achieve "fairness" one spouse should be "compensated" for a loss or disadvantage generated from the marriage, for example. This can occur where one spouse has sacrificed their career for the benefit of the family, however the concept of compensation has found less favour in recent years and the circumstances where such an argument is likely to be successful are quite rare.

The concept of compensation was born in the case of ***McFarlane,*** where the wife had given up a highly lucrative career in order to care for the parties' children. The husband continued with his career from which he was receiving significant income which left the parties with a large surplus even after both parties ongoing needs had been met. Rather than ascribe a "need" to the wife for a proportion of the surplus income with which to make provision for her retirement, as the husband was able to do for his own, the court considered that the wife was entitled to be compensated for the loss that she had suffered arising from the marriage.

In ***VB v JP (2008)***[43] Potter P gave guidance in respect of the concept of compensation into the generosity of the interpretation of needs[44].

In ***Waggott***[45], the Court of Appeal proposed a test for applying the compensation principle. First, the court should determine, using the civil burden, that the applicant's career would have resulted in them having greater resources than those which they would be awarded under either the needs or the sharing principles. The court must then decide whether and if so, how, compensation should be reflected to

---

[43] EWHC 112 (fam)

[44] Para 59

[45] *Wagott v Waggott (2018) EWCA Civ 727*

ensure fairness to both parties. This suggests that a more flexible approach to determining compensation may be appropriate in some cases, than generous assessment of a spouses ongoing needs.

In the recent case of ***RC v JC (2020)***[46] a claim for compensation was successfully argued. In this case, the wife gave up her chance to become a partner in the law firm in which she worked, in order that the husband's career could take priority. The compensation in this case was awarded to the wife with a separate lump sum of £400,000, in addition to an equal share of the assets of £4.85 million, on a clean break basis. Her award comprised of £2.5 million for housing and £2.35 million as a Duxbury fund, based on joint lives periodical payments of £100,00 per annum. The £400,000 compensation award was predicated 4 further years of periodical payments, during which the husband was expected to continue working. Moor J emphasized that compensation awards were rare, however in this case, the assets were sufficient to fund the claim after a sharing award had been made and needs met. Furthermore, there was documentary evidence which supported the wife's contention in respect of her capabilities and career prospects.

Sharing

We have established that where the resources of the parties exceed their reasonable needs, the application of the sharing principle will generally lead to an equal sharing of the matrimonial assets.

Where there is genuine non-matrimonial property, it is unlikely to be subject to the sharing principle, however it is possible that it could be, in circumstances where it has been "matrimonialised" by being placed into the parties' joint names or used to purchase a holiday home which is enjoyed by the family, for example. Generally, in big money cases,

---

[46] *JC v RC (2020) EWHC 466 (fam)*

needs will always be met in full and generously interpreted. As such, it is unlikely that any further consideration of needs will be required. However, in big money cases in which the assets are mostly or entirely non-matrimonial in nature, so that the sharing principle is barely engaged, if at all, the application will be determined entirely on the basis of needs of the applicant spouse, having regard to all of the other s25 factors.

Summary

- Needs will generally trump most arguments in a case, irrespective of the duration of the marriage.

- Assets built up during the course of the marriage are likely to be subject to the sharing principle, unless needs dictates otherwise.

- The length of a marriage does not impact upon the sharing principle. The court should not distinguish between an accrual over a short marriage and an accrual over a longer marriage.

- In some circumstances, consideration may be given as to whether to achieve "fairness" one spouse should be "compensated" for a loss or disadvantage generated from the marriage, for example. The concept of compensation has found less favour in recent years and the circumstances where such an argument is likely to be successful, are fairly rare.

CHAPTER SIX

FUTURE NEEDS OF THE CHILDREN AND THE PARTIES

We will now consider how the court has approached the needs of the children and the parties in a short marriage. We will start with the somewhat exceptional *pre- White* case **of** ***C v C (1997)***[47]**.**

The facts

In this case, in the space of just over nine months, the parties married, had a child and subsequently separated. Following separation, the wife issued divorce proceedings and made an application for financial remedy, the outcome of which was that the husband was ordered to pay:

1. A lump sum of £195,000 for housing;
2. Periodical payments at the rate of £19,500 on a joint lives basis;
3. Child maintenance at the rate of £8000 per annum.

It was also ordered that the husband's property should be charged by way of security in respect of the periodical payments. The husband appealed, on the grounds that:

1. The capital award was too generous to the wife;

---

[47] *C v C (1997) 2 FLR 26*

2. Any lump sum should be settled on the child during his minority, with reversion to the husband (akin to a schedule 1[48] scenario);

3. The quantum of periodical payments was too high and a term of two years should be imposed;

4. There was no need for the periodical payments to be secured.

The husband's appeal was dismissed. Ward LJ said that although the marriage was very short, it had profound and continuing consequences for the wife's earning capacity, in the short to medium term and therefore the first instance award was appropriate.

Ward LJ found that although the periodical payments award was high, the same did not fall outside of the scope of reasonableness. The test regarding the term of the same was whether it should be confined to such a term as would be sufficient to enable the wife to adjust without undue hardship to the termination of financial dependence on the husband. Appropriateness could be measured against all of the s25 criteria, including the welfare of the child. Ward LJ considered that it was not appropriate to impose a term simply because this was a short marriage. He felt that there was too much uncertainty in the wife's position going forward and that in any case, the husband could always seek a variation in the future. Ward LJ also found that while it might appear that the provision for the wife was overly generous when considering the brevity of the marriage, the total amount awarded was at the very top of the bracket, but it was a bracket in which he had a vast discretion, which the judge at first instance was entitled to exercise.

---

[48] *Schedule 1 Children Act 1989*

Ward LJ set out 8 points, a – h in his judgement at paragraphs 42c – 46e, in which he summarised the "proper approach"

(a) The first task is for the court to consider a clean break.

(b) If there is to be no clean break, then what is the amount to be ordered. The duration of the marriage is a factor relevant when deciding quantum.

(c) If a periodical payments order is made, the court must then consider whether to impose a term.

(d) The court then must ask itself if it is appropriate to order pp's only for a term.

(e) What is "appropriate" depends on all the circumstances of the case. It is not appropriate simply to say, "this is a short marriage, therefore a term must be imposed".

(f) when considering the making of a periodical payments order, the court should consider the duration of the marriage, the need to care for any children and the effect that will have on the earning capacity of the receiving party. It should within that, consider any difficulties they may have in going back to work.

(g) The court cannot decide that a term is appropriate, without evidence to support its conclusion. Crystal ball gazing is not sufficient.

(h) Finally, the court must also be satisfied that the recipient will adjust within the term that is fixed. The court may be in a position of such certainty that it can impose a Section 28(1A) bar.

The decision of Ward LJ in ***C v C*** must however be considered in the context of more recent decisions. Mostyn J has since emphasised that in a short marriage case, the discretion when assessing needs is particularly broad and fact sensitive and there is no rule or guideline to the effect that income needs should be met by the making of a term order[49].

B v B (2002)[50] emphasised that even in a short marriage, the future needs of any children must be considered.

The facts

In this case, significant (relative to the assets) indefinite periodical payments and a lump sum for housing needs were awarded to the wife, leaving the husband short of capital, after a marriage of less than a year, with one small child. Munby J found that although the marriage was of a short duration, the wife would effectively have to contribute to the marriage for the next two decades in bringing up the child, and that her earning capacity would suffer, while the husband's large earning capacity meant that he would easily be able to rebuild his finances.

Referring to ***C v C,*** Munby J referred to what Ward LJ had identified as the proper approach. He emphasised that in the financial analysis the decision had, of necessity, to depend on all of the circumstances of the case, including the welfare of the child and the section 25 criteria. In respect of the maintenance award, he referred to Ward's comments and concluded that while it was a short marriage, it was not the case that a term ought to be imposed in respect of the maintenance award.

---

[49] *FF v KF (2017) EWHC 1093 (Fam) (2017) All ER D 94*

[50] *B v B (2002) 1 FLR 555*

In ***McCartney v Mills McCartney (2008)***[51] It was established that needs after a short marriage should generally be viewed less generously than after a long marriage.

The facts

The husband, Paul McCartney, had accumulated non-matrimonial assets in the order of £400 million. There was virtually no marital acquest. The parties plainly enjoyed a very high standard of living during their marriage of about 4 years. There was one child of the marriage, whose needs were being met separately by the husband. The wife sought a lump sum in excess of £125 million. Conversely, the husband proposed that the wife exit the marriage with a lump sum of £15 million, after a deduction for conduct.

Bennet J awarded the wife a lump sum of £16.5 million, giving the wife total assets of £24.3 million. The following factors led to his decision:

- The brevity of the marriage
- The significant non-matrimonial property brought into the marriage by the husband
- The almost total absence of any marital acquest

Bennet J said in his judgement:

> *"In a case where the vast bulk of the husband's enormous fortune was made not only before their marriage but also indeed before the wife and husband even met; where the*

---

[51] *McCartney v Mills – McCartney (2008) EWHC 401 (Fam) (2008) 1 FLR 508*

> *"marital acquest" (if such there has been) is of a very small amount compared to the total assets; where the compensation principle is not in any way engaged; where the marriage is short and where the standard of living lasted only so long as the marriage; where the wife is now and will be very comfortably housed; and where [the child's] needs are fully assured, surely fairness requires that the wife's needs (generously interpreted) are the dominant factor in the section 25 exercise. Any other radically different way of looking at this case would, in my judgment, be manifestly unfair."*[52]

The award to Ms Mills was then and remains the largest needs-based awards in any reported case. This was clearly an exceptional case and as such, it would be wrong to assume that a needs-led award will always follow in a short marriage case. The principles of sharing and equality apply as much in short marriages as they do in those of longer duration. As family practitioners, we will all be aware that some damage limitation can be carried out, if a prenuptial agreement is entered into prior to the marriage. This would demonstrate the clear intention of the parties as to how their finances should be dealt with in the event of the breakdown of the marriage.

Summary

- Case law continues to emphasise the width of discretion the court has in applying the s25 factors. As circumstances vary to significantly from case to case, it is often difficult to establish clear and consistent principles.

---

[52] Para 311

- The presence of children will clearly have a bearing on a financial remedy award, since the future needs of the children and the parties will have to be met.

- The presence of children in a marriage will not be relevant to the sharing principle.

CHAPTER SEVEN

SHORT, CHILDLESS MARRIAGES

Sharp v Sharp (2017)[53]

Even where the marriage is very short, if the parties have children, the court's approach will be different to a case where the marriage was short and childless.

The facts

The parties were in their forties and their relationship lasted for around 6 years. There were no children of the marriage. They began cohabiting in 2007 and subsequently married in 2009. The wife issued divorce proceedings in December 2013, following the husband's affair. Both parties came from relatively modest financial backgrounds. The husband worked in IT and the wife was a trader. In the early stages of their cohabitation, they had similar salaries of about £100,000 per annum, however the wife received significant bonuses that amounted to about £10.5 million during their relationship. In 2008 the wife utilised her funds to purchase the parties first property in joint names for £1.02 million. In 2012 she funded the purchase of a second property, also in the parties' joint names for £2 million. The husband took voluntary redundancy in order to project manage refurbishment work at their second property, although the wife later argued that he had exaggerated this role. Following separation, the husband lived at the first property and the wife the second. Throughout the course of the marriage, the parties kept their finances

[53] Foster v Foster (2003) EWCA Civ 565

mostly separate, albeit there was no deliberate intention to operate in this way. At the time of the first hearing, the parties' total assets were £6.9 million. The wife offered the husband £1.23 million, representing the transfer to him of their first property and a lump sum of £130,000 for legal fees. The husband sought an award of £3 million.

Singer J held that there should be equal sharing of the assets that were built up during the marriage, regardless of its duration or the parties' contributions. The sharing principle would therefore apply. Singer J assumed a figure of £5.45 million, which was calculated by excluding the first property from the total assets of £6.9 million, on the basis that it was acquired by the wife before the parties married and a further £350,000 in respect of other pre-acquired assets. An equal division of £5.45 million provided the husband with £2.725 million. Singer J awarded the husband £2.725m, exactly 50% of the matrimonial assets after deductions and the husband's concessions regarding one of the properties. Singer J when considering whether the sharing principle applies, concluded that:

> *'It is in my judgment consistent with current principle that the matrimonial acquest that the value of the assets and savings built up during the marriage, irrespective of the very different proportions in which the parties contributed to them, should be subject to the equal sharing principle.*

The wife subsequently appealed the decision, on the basis that this was a short, dual career, childless marriage and therefore the sharing principle should be relaxed. Further, the parties had kept their finances mostly separate. The wife proposed that the assets for division should be confined to the respective net value of the two properties, being £2.6 million. This would provide the husband with £1.3 million and the wife would retain her other separately held assets. The husband argued that other than special contribution or non-matrimonial assets, all of the assets should be divided equally between the parties, regardless of the brevity of the marriage or the fact that the parties had kept their finances separate.

McFarlane LJ awarded the husband £2 million, comprising £1.1 million, being the value of the first property and a lump sum of £900,000. The rationale being that the husband should have half of the combined value of the two properties (£1.3 million) and receive an award of £700,000 to reflect the following factors

- The standard of living enjoyed by the parties during the marriage
- The need for a small capital fund to enable the husband to live comfortably in the first property
- A share in some of the assets held by the wife

McFarlane LJ noted that:

- there was a fringe of cases that may fall outside of the sharing principle established in White that applies to the vast majority of decisions;
- the application of an equal split in every case would be an impermissible gloss on the statute, which expressly requires the court to consider all of the circumstances of a case, including the duration of the marriage;
- In Miller, Baroness Hale, Lord Mance and Lord Hoffman concluded that consideration of departing from the sharing principle in order to achieve fairness, in so far as there were separately held assets in a short, dual career marriage and their majority view should have been followed;

- The obiter comments of the Court of Appeal in Charman[54] should not have been considered to be a definitive statement of the law in which there was suggestion that the sharing principle applies fully to short marriages.

- Singer J's analysis could not be reconciled with the majority opinion in Miller that equal sharing applies to separately held assets even in a short marriage case, where needs are met.

- Singer J's view that the sharing principle would apply unless the parties had entered into a pre-nuptial agreement was not supported by any authority.

The decision of the Court of Appeal highlights that the sharing principle will be engaged in the vast majority of cases, but there is no automatic presumption of an equal division of assets. The court must apply the s25 factors in order to achieve a fair outcome. In a small minority of cases, a short marriage where there are no children, dual career and separate finances may justify a departure from equality in order to achieve fairness. McFarlane LJ iterated that absent sound principles, the determination of a fair financial outcome would require a fact-specific case-by-case analysis.

At paragraph 97 of his judgement, having considered ***Miller v Miller; McFarlane v McFarlane***, he said:

> *"...rather than a strict application of the equal sharing principle in relation to short childless marriages, where both spouses have largely been in full time employment and where only some of their finances have been pooled...fairness may require a reduction from a full 50% share or the exclusion of some property from the 50% calculation".*

54 Para 86

The issue for determination was whether it was *inevitable* that matrimonial assets should be shared equally, where the marriage was short; childless; and the couple had both worked and maintained separate finances; and one had earned substantial bonuses.

The Court of Appeal held that, as a matter of principle, fairness may require a reduction from a full 50% share or the exclusion of some property from the 50% calculation. ***Miller*** had established that departure from the principle of equal sharing may occur in order to achieve the overarching goal of fairness in a particular case. The Court of Appeal determined that the manner in which the parties arranged their finances in this case was more than sufficient to establish that the wife had maintained her capital separately in a manner that was compatible with that described in ***Miller***. Accordingly, the division of the assets determined by the judge did not accord with the approach dictated by the majority in ***Miller***.

As noted above, McFarlane LJ emphasised that absent sound principles, the determination of a fair financial income would quickly result in a fact-specific case by cased analysis, likely to result in emotional and financial cost to the parties, without significant benefit to them or society in general. However, the decision does raise questions that are likely to lead to further legal arguments about what constitutes a short marriage and the period following which wealth generated in the marriage, should be shared equally. The decision illustrates that a pre-nuptial agreement may not be needed to avoid equal sharing of assets built up during a marriage that is short, childless and where both parties work and keep their finances separate. However, a pre-nuptial agreement in these circumstances may of course, provide greater certainty to the parties and obviate the need for litigation and the concomitant costs attached.

Sharp was one of the rare cases where identified factors justified a departure from the equal sharing principle. It was confirmed that, pursuant to ***Miller***, as a matter of principle, fairness may require a departure from equality in dividing matrimonial assets, even where there are assets surplus to needs, on the basis of s.25(2)(f), where one party has made an unmatched contribution to the marriage. As we have seen, these are rare cases, though perhaps less rare in short, childless marriages than in long marriages.

FF v KF (2017)[55]

The facts

In this case, Mostyn J gives guidance on the discretion to be exercised by a judge in respect of how needs should be assessed in a short, childless marriage.

The parties married when the husband was 63 and the wife was 36. They commenced their relationship in 2004. They became engaged and a wedding ceremony was fixed for 27 December 2007. However, three days before the ceremony the husband called the wedding off, with the consequence that the wife, who is Ukrainian, had to leave the country. In October 2010 the parties rekindled their relationship. They resumed cohabitation in April 2011. They married in Las Vegas on 3 October 2011. They separated on 23 September 2013. Therefore, the actual marriage was for less than two years, although the most recent period of cohabitation was for 2½ years. However, the parties' relationship spanned over nine years, with a separation of three years in between.

The husband had amassed a considerable amount of premarital wealth. The wife suffered psychological harm as a result of the marriage and its breakdown and left the marriage very damaged and vulnerable, with her future/earning capacity being uncertain. At the final hearing it was ordered that the wife should have a lump sum of

[55] *FF v KF (2017) EWHC 1093*

£4.25m on a clean break basis, which would be a housing fund, plus enable her to discharge her debts and provide a capitalised income fund to her for a term.

The husband appealed. The argument advanced on his behalf was that the judge's discretion had miscarried, in that he had gone beyond an assessment of the wife's needs and had taken into account unspecified factors.

The High Court dismissed the appeal, holding that the wife's immediate capital needs and future income needs were within the judge's discretion to ascertain. The judge was generous, but the award had fallen within the legitimate bracket.

As per Mostyn J: '*So far as the "needs" principle is concerned there is an almost unbounded discretion. The main rule is that, save in a situation of real hardship, the "needs" must be causally related to the marriage….In a short marriage case the discretion when assessing needs is particularly broad and fact-sensitive…*' [para 18].

Mostyn J iterated that need was a relative concept, as long as "*the judge's foot*" [para 18]. Needs is "*a term of art*", assessment of which is a discretionary exercise of the payer's wealth, the length of the marriage, the applicant's age and health, and the standard of living.

In short, childless marriages, it will often be the case that a financially weaker spouse does not have any recourse to the non-matrimonial wealth of the other party. However, where there are needs generated by the marriage, these must be met, even if this means resorting to non-matrimonial wealth. It is up to the judge to interpret those needs as they see fit. As such, there are cases in which a short, childless marriage, with non-matrimonial 'big money' may result in a departure from equality.

This judgement reminds practitioners that in many short marriage cases, income needs are determined by making a term order, although there is no authority to this effect. We have seen that joint lives support was awarded after a short marriage in ***C v C***[56] and at first instance in ***M v M***[57] in which the House of Lords upheld the decision in ***Miller***.

> "*Since the decision of the House of Lords in Miller v Miller [2006] UKHL 24, [2006] 2 AC 618 these cases are now decided by the parallel application of the two principles of sharing and needs (compensation has never yet played a part in any case, and in my opinion is unlikely ever to do so). The authorities make clear, and common-sense dictates, that the result is the higher of the two figures generated by the principles. So, if the sharing principle produces a figure of £1 million but the needs principle produces a figure of £4 million then the result is £4 million. Equivalently, if the needs principle produces a figure of £1 million but the sharing principle produces a figure of £4 million then the result, again, is £4 million. There is no warrant for suggesting, when one has arrived at the higher of the two figures generated by the principles, that one can augment it by further unspecified factors; and it is impossible to believe, as this is so well known, that the judge could have intended otherwise. Further, these phrases of the judge are in fact meaningless in the context of the decision that he rendered. The battle lines were drawn exclusively by reference to need, and his decision, when analysed, is clearly based on the application of that principle*"[58]

---

[56] (1997) 2 FLR 26

[57] (2005) EWHC 528 (fam)

[58] Para 17

> *"So far as the "needs" principle is concerned there is an almost unbounded discretion. The main rule is that save in a situation of real hardship, the "needs" must be causally related to the marriage. Like equity in the old days, the result seems to depend on the length of the judge's foot. It is worth recalling that Heather Mills-McCartney was awarded over £25m to meet her "needs" (**McCartney v McCartney [2008] EWHC 401 (Fam)**). Mrs Juffali was awarded £62m to meet her "needs" (**Juffali v Juffali [2016] EWHC 1684 (Fam)**). In the very recent case of **AAZ v BBZ [2016] EWHC 3234 (Fam)** the court assessed the applicant-wife's "needs" in the remarkable sum of £224m. Plainly "needs" does not mean needs. It is a term of art. Obviously, no-one actually <u>needs</u> £25m, or £62m, or £224m for accommodation and sustenance. The main drivers in the discretionary exercise are the scale of the payer's wealth, the length of the marriage, the applicant's age and health, and the standard of living, although the latter factor cannot be allowed to dominate the exercise".*[59]

This case reaffirms and highlights the broad width of discretion judges have when assessing a parties' needs.

In ***E v L (2021)***[60] Mostyn J provides clear guidance on whether a childless or short marriage justifies a departure from the equal sharing principle and gives information on the valuation of business assets. We will of course, focus on the principles established in the judgement concerning the relationship between short, childless marriage and the sharing principle.

---

[59] Para 18

[60] E v L (2021) EWFC 60 (Fam)

The facts

The husband was 66 and the wife 61. Their relationship commenced in 2015 and the husband immediately began providing the wife with financial support, paying her between £5,000 and £10,000 per month. The parties became engaged in 2016, married in 2017 and separated in 2019. The parties disagreed in respect of the dates of cohabitation, with the wife asserting that the same began in 2016 and the husband denying that there was any cohabitation at all, prior to the marriage.

The husband was a highly successful production manager for live music events, specialising in audio and visual effects. The husband had reached the pinnacle of his career in this industry, working with a well -known artist on their world tour between 2017 – 2019, which was one of the highest grossing concerts of all time. Over the course of his career, he had worked with some of the biggest names in music. The husband had an interest in six different companies. There was a significant dispute in respect of the value of company A. The value of the husband's interest in the other companies was of no relevance to the outcome of the case. The wife sought a lump sum of £5.5 million in accordance with her calculation of half of the matrimonial assets. The husband's open position was that he should pay the wife just £600,000, on the basis of the brevity of the marriage, the fact that there were no children, the fact that it was not in his view, a sharing case and furthermore, the wife's needs ought to be conservatively assessed.

The judge identified that "*the extent of the difference between the parties is extraordinary. It seems to be the production of the imprecision within the case – law combined with the intransigence and dogmatism by the parties in pursuit and defence of the claim*".

Since the application of the sharing principle looks at the value accrued during the course of the marital relationship and deems the parties' incommensurable contributions to that accrual to be of equal value, then divides that equally, why should the presence of a child make any difference?

In ***Sharp***[61], McFarlane stated:

> *"The inescapable conclusion from this analysis of the speeches in Miller, in terms of the possibility of some alteration from, rather than a strict application of, the equal sharing principle in relation to short, childless marriages, where both spouses have largely been in full-time employment and where only some of their finances have been pooled, is that fairness may require a reduction from a full 50% share or the exclusion of some property from the 50% calculation. Of the five members of the Judicial Committee, only Lord Nicholls suggested a contrary view and even on his analysis the potential for some form of relaxation can be seen"*

And in ***XW v XH***[62] Moylan LJ, seemingly accepted that the sharing principle could apply in a short marriage case which was childless, stated:

> *"141. Returning to Miller, in my view, the substantive focus of Lady Hale's observations, at [147] to [153], is short, childless marriages. However, even if she left open that they might apply in other than such marriages, we can now see that to apply them to those cases would be discriminatory in the same way that special contributions initially risked being applied in a way which would have significantly undermined the progress made by White.*

---

[61] *Sharp v Sharp 2017 EWCA Civ 40*

[62] *(2019) EWCA Civ 2262*

142. Whilst there may be elements within the above paragraphs in Miller which are capable of a broader interpretation, I am persuaded that they do not require this court to take that approach. I acknowledge, in this discretionary area, that it would be unwise to close doors to the notion that fairness might leave scope for the court to decide not to effect an equal division of marital assets because of a particular factor or combination of factors in an individual case. However, as a matter of general principle, I find it hard to envisage how, in other than short, childless marriages fairness would be achieved if the existence of "business assets" *was the basis of justifying anything other than equal division.*

145. Accordingly, it is evident that a broader application of a different approach to a marital asset merely because it was a business asset would be, as was identified in Charman, at [83], ***"deeply discriminatory"*** *and would, therefore,* ***"gravely undermine the sharing principle"*** *The effect would be the same whether property is excluded from the sharing principle, because it is not treated as marital property, or whether the sharing principle is not applied to such property so as to divide it equally. Indeed, it would seem to me likely to be rare for sufficient wealth to have been generated other than through "business efforts and acumen" for the determinative principle to be sharing rather than need. This is why I have concluded that the application of a different approach to the business assets, in other than a short, childless marriage, would result in the sharing principle being undermined in the same way identified in Charman and, accordingly, that the judge was wrong to take this factor into account, at [239].* (Emphasis added)

The husband argued that childlessness is indicative of an entirely different category of commitment. This argument was squarely rejected by the judge.

When applying the sharing principle *"for the court to start asking why there are no children, and whether this denotes a lesser extent of commitment to the relationship, is to make windows into people's souls, and should be avoided at all costs."* [29]

On an analysis of ***Miller***, Mostyn J found that childlessness was not one of the reasons why the House of Lords upheld the unequal division of the acquest in that case [31] and it was unclear how this factor had crept into *Sharp* [33].

And at [34] *"In my judgement this factor should be banished from any consideration of whether there should be a departure from the application of the sharing principle. Whatever may be the true construction of that section of Baroness Hale's speech, it does not include bringing into consideration the childlessness of the marriage, if that were the case. "*

In relation to the application of the sharing principle to short marriages as to long marriages the judge stated with reference to his opinion in ***GW v RW [2003] 2FLR 108*** that in order to have equal validity with a financial contribution, a domestic contribution needed to be earned over time *"I now figuratively hold my hand in the flames and recant. There is absolutely no logical reason to draw a distinction between an accrual over a short period and an accrual over a long period. As Lord Nicholls pointed out (Miller), that statutory factor of the duration of the marriage will be reflected in the nature of things by the fact that in a short marriage the accrual will almost inevitably be less than in a longer marriage "[43]*

We have seen how there is of course the possible rare exception to this in respect of non- matrimonial assets generated by one spouse alone during a short marriage, where those assets have been kept separate and where both spouses have been financially independent. It is for this reason that the Court of Appeal in ***Sharp***[63] acknowledged the exception[64] but confirmed that the exception would only apply in the minority of cases.

Mostyn J held that the reason for the rarity was obvious. "*The exception is founded on the notion that the value of the contributions made by one spouse during a short marriage in generating "business assets" is worth more than the value of the contributions made by the other spouse during that period. Like the now discredited doctrine of special contributions this notion gives rise to the Orwellian oxymoron that all contributions are equal but some are more equal than others. It is very difficult to escape the conclusion that discriminatory forces are underpinning this notion. Hence the need to confine the application to extremely rare situations*"[65]

Excluding non- matrimonial property does not however involve a departure from the sharing principle in that "*this is plainly a legitimate technique to apply in any case, but most particularly in a short marriage case where the connections and transactions happened relatively recently and have not faded into the past with the result that the fruits of the transaction became matrimonialised*"[66]

The court awarded the wife with half of the matrimonial assets (post costs) and ordered the husband to pay a lump sum of £1,515,000 on a clean break basis.

63 Sharp v Sharp (2017) EWCA Civ 408

64 Para 44

65 Para 46

66 Para 50

"There is no good reason to at all to depart from equality in the division. This case is not a white leopard"[67]

The rationale for the decision was as follows:

(a) A marriage is a marriage, childlessness should be banished from any consideration of whether there should be a departure from the application of the equal sharing principle.

(b) There is no logical reason to draw a distinction between an accrual of assets over a short period and a long period. The duration of the marriage [s.25(2)(d)] will be reflected anyway as accrual in a short marriage will almost inevitably be less than in a longer marriage. Though *Miller* allowed for a rare exception in departing from equality, this should be very narrowly confined to avoid undermining the sharing principle.

Note, however, that this does not mean that non-matrimonial wealth should be shared – this can and often *should* be retained by the party who accrued it.

(c) Save in cases where there has been undue delay between the separation and placing of the matter before the court, the end date for the purposes of calculation of the acquest should be the date of trial.

(d) The duration of the marriage impacts forcefully and directly on the assessment of need – needs are likely to be less generously interpreted, and the standard of living enjoyed

[67] Para 77

during the marriage is likely to be less persuasive, when a marriage is short.

Summary

- The presence of children does not impact upon the level of commitment between the parties and justify a departure from the equal sharing principle.
- The presence of children within a marriage is only relevant to needs, rather than the sharing principle.
- A *Miller*-style departure from equality is not a given in short, childless marriages that have not generated particular needs.
- The *Miller* exception cannot be allowed to creep towards a wider application. It is relevant to a very narrow selection of cases and should not undermine the sharing principle or allow discrimination in by the backdoor.
- There is no rule or guideline that income needs following a short marriage are to be determined by a term order.
- Needs following a short childless marriage should be conservatively assessed.

CHAPTER EIGHT

CONCLUSION – WHERE DOES THIS LEAVE US?

Duration of the marriage

The duration of the marriage can have a significant impact upon the outcome of a case. It is just one of the many factors the court must consider when undertaking the s25 assessment. In the context of short marriages, the very strict approach taken in ***Krystman***[68] is likely to be confined to its facts, and the law has developed significantly since. The concept of 'reasonable requirements' is a thing of the past.

As family practitioners, we should not become too concerned with whether a marriage is 'short' or 'childless' insofar as the same principles (s25 factors) apply to marriages regardless of length or children.

We have seen how case law continues to emphasise the width of discretion the court has in applying the s25 factors. As circumstances vary so significantly from case to case, it is often difficult to establish clear and consistent principles. What is clear, is that the relevance of each of the s25(2) factors varies from case to case.

Premarital cohabitation

It is now generally accepted that any premarital cohabitation will be added to the length of the marriage when the court assess the duration of the marriage. The prevailing view is that the commencement of cohabitation in a settled relationship can be treated as the appropriate

---

[68] *Krystman v Krystman (1973) All ER 247*

start date. This approach reflects changes in social habits, in that now many people choose to live together prior to marriage or civil partnership.

Where there has been a period of seamless cohabitation before the marriage, that period of time is also added to the length of the marriage. Therefore, in many circumstances, and particularly for younger couples who are more likely to live together these days prior to marriage, the relevant consideration for family lawyers would be when the parties started living together, as opposed to when they got married or registered their civil partnership.

Relationship after marriage

The period following the breakdown of the marriage is also a relevant consideration for the court. The pertinent consideration is therefore the date of separation as opposed to the date of the final decree. It may be that although the marriage breaks down, the parties remain emotionally enmeshed with each other. If this is the case, the court might consider it inappropriate to ignore the period during which they continue to be involved. With regard to the end of a marriage or civil partnership, it is now more common for the court to look at the date of separation rather than the date of the final decree. As we can see from ***MB v EB***[69] however, each case will turn on its unique facts and the application of the s25 factors will ultimately determine the appropriate outcome. Any post – marital cohabitation is likely to be treated in the same way as premarital cohabitation, per ***S v S***[70].

[69] *MB v EB (2019) EWHC 1649*

[70] *S v S (1994) 2 FLR 228*

The sharing principle

Matrimonial property falls to be shared, whether the marriage is long or short. Where the parties' relationship is short and there are no children of the family, the court will generally consider that an equal division of all assets accrued during the relationship would be appropriate.

There should be no discrimination between the parties on the basis of their respective roles or that one earns more than the other. The marriage and its financial success is regarded a joint enterprise, which the parties should share in equally. The fact that a marriage is a short one is irrelevant to how the matrimonial assets should be divided. s25 factors are applied equally (without any one factor predominating) when dividing the matrimonial property from a short marriage.

Where both parties have brough similar wealth into the marriage, have similar incomes and there are no children of the family, the court's aim is likely to be to restore each party to the financial positions they were each in before they married.

Needs

Needs generated by the marriage will be addressed, by reference to matrimonial assets or non-matrimonial assets where required as per ***FF v KF.*** Though note that needs are likely to be less generously interpreted, and the standard of living enjoyed during the marriage is likely to be less persuasive, when a marriage is short ***E v L.*** It should be noted, however, that a departure from equality may be more likely in a short and/or childless marriage insofar as –

(a) non-matrimonial wealth may be easier to distinguish from matrimonial wealth as in ***Foster,*** and;

(b) an unmatched contribution to matrimonial wealth may be harder to establish where there are children, compared to cases of childless marriages, as in ***Miller*** **and *Sharp*.**

Contributions and non-matrimonial property

When the marriage has been short and if assets were owned solely by one party prior to the marriage or relationship, then they are less likely to be divided on an equal basis. In those circumstances, it is more likely that the party that brough the asset into the marriage will retain it, or at least a greater share of it, unless there are compelling needs-based arguments to the contrary.

It is possible to depart from the principle of equality where one individual has made an overwhelming contribution to a short marriage. The sharing principle applies to the matrimonial assets of a short marriage as much as a long marriage as per ***Foster***, with the 'yardstick of equality' acting a point of reference. It is possible to have a substantial departure from equal division of matrimonial property per ***Miller***, where this is appropriate due to the unmatched contributions made by one party, coupled with other factors such as the way that the parties have managed/separated their finances, as per ***Sharp***. Nonetheless, the ***Miller*** principle needs to be narrowly interpreted and applied, in order to prevent the sharing principle from being undermined, as per ***E v L***. Sharing of non- matrimonial property absent a needs-based argument is extremely rare. ***Sharp*** was one of the rare cases where identified factors justified departure from the equal sharing principle. It was confirmed that, pursuant to ***Miller***, as a matter of principle, fairness may require a departure from equality in dividing matrimonial assets, even where there are assets over and above needs. This is on the basis of s25(2)(f), where one party has made an unequal contribution. As we have seen, these are rare cases, though perhaps less rare in short, childless marriages than in long marriages.

Following ***Sharp*** the court has been emphatic in stating that the retention of personal wealth should not come at the expense of meeting a spouse's reasonable needs. The length of the marriage and the quantum of wealth over needs, has made it easier for the court to separate matrimonial from non- matrimonial property and to apply s25 strictly to the matrimonial property.

Term order?

A clean break is more likely to be deemed appropriate where the length of the marriage is short, although a clean break is not a foregone conclusion, simply because the marriage is short. As with the early case of ***C v C***, the principle is echoed in ***FF v KF*** that a short marriage will not necessarily result in a term order.

And finally…

Within this book there is much reference to the leading case law and established jurisprudence in respect of the court's approach to short marriages. While this is all incredibly important, ultimately, and irrespective of whether you are dealing with a short, medium or long-term marriage, if you apply each of the s25 criteria to your case, you cannot go wrong! It is clear that the court's approach to a short marriage case and the application of the s25 criteria is the same regardless of the duration of the marriage, although as we have established throughout the course of this book, the outcome of these cases can be quite different, when the marriage has been short.

MORE BOOKS BY LAW BRIEF PUBLISHING

'A Practical Guide to Religion and Belief Discrimination Claims in the Workplace' by Kashif Ali
'A Practical Guide to the Law of Medical Treatment Decisions' by Ben Troke
'Fundamental Dishonesty and QOCS in Personal Injury Proceedings: Law and Practice' by Jake Rowley
'A Practical Guide to the Law in Relation to School Exclusions' by Charlotte Hadfield & Alice de Coverley
'A Practical Guide to Divorce for the Silver Separators' by Karin Walker
'The Right to be Forgotten – The Law and Practical Issues' by Melissa Stock
'A Practical Guide to Planning Law and Rights of Way in National Parks, the Broads and AONBs' by James Maurici QC, James Neill et al
'A Practical Guide to Election Law' by Tom Tabori
'A Practical Guide to the Law in Relation to Surrogacy' by Andrew Powell
'A Practical Guide to Claims Arising from Fatal Accidents – 2nd Edition' by James Patience
'A Practical Guide to the Ownership of Employee Inventions – From Entitlement to Compensation' by James Tumbridge & Ashley Roughton
'A Practical Guide to Asbestos Claims' by Jonathan Owen & Gareth McAloon
'A Practical Guide to Stamp Duty Land Tax in England and Northern Ireland' by Suzanne O'Hara
'A Practical Guide to the Law of Farming Partnerships' by Philip Whitcomb
'Covid-19, Homeworking and the Law – The Essential Guide to Employment and GDPR Issues' by Forbes Solicitors
'Covid-19 and Criminal Law – The Essential Guide' by Ramya Nagesh
'Covid-19 and Family Law in England and Wales – The Essential Guide' by Safda Mahmood
'A Practical Guide to the Law of Unlawful Eviction and Harassment – 2nd Edition' by Stephanie Lovegrove
'Covid-19, Brexit and the Law of Commercial Leases – The Essential Guide' by Mark Shelton
'A Practical Guide to Costs in Personal Injury Claims – 2nd Edition' by Matthew Hoe

'A Practical Guide to the General Data Protection Regulation (GDPR) – 2nd Edition' by Keith Markham
'Ellis on Credit Hire – Sixth Edition' by Aidan Ellis & Tim Kevan
'A Practical Guide to Working with Litigants in Person and McKenzie Friends in Family Cases' by Stuart Barlow
'Protecting Unregistered Brands: A Practical Guide to the Law of Passing Off' by Lorna Brazell
'A Practical Guide to Secondary Liability and Joint Enterprise Post-Jogee' by Joanne Cecil & James Mehigan
'A Practical Guide to the Pre-Action RTA Claims Protocol for Personal Injury Lawyers' by Antonia Ford
'A Practical Guide to Neighbour Disputes and the Law' by Alexander Walsh
'A Practical Guide to Forfeiture of Leases' by Mark Shelton
'A Practical Guide to Coercive Control for Legal Practitioners and Victims' by Rachel Horman
'A Practical Guide to Rights Over Airspace and Subsoil' by Daniel Gatty
'Tackling Disclosure in the Criminal Courts – A Practitioner's Guide' by Narita Bahra QC & Don Ramble
'A Practical Guide to the Law of Driverless Cars – Second Edition' by Alex Glassbrook, Emma Northey & Scarlett Milligan
'A Practical Guide to TOLATA Claims' by Greg Williams
'A Practical Guide to Elderly Law – 2nd Edition' by Justin Patten
'A Practical Guide to the Law of Prescription in Scotland' by Andrew Foyle
'A Practical Guide to the Construction and Rectification of Wills and Trust Instruments' by Edward Hewitt
'A Practical Guide to the Law of Bullying and Harassment in the Workplace' by Philip Hyland
'How to Be a Freelance Solicitor: A Practical Guide to the SRA-Regulated Freelance Solicitor Model' by Paul Bennett
'A Practical Guide to Prison Injury Claims' by Malcolm Johnson
'A Practical Guide to the Small Claims Track - 2nd Edition' by Dominic Bright
'A Practical Guide to Advising Clients at the Police Station' by Colin Stephen McKeown-Beaumont

'A Practical Guide to Antisocial Behaviour Injunctions' by Iain Wightwick
'Practical Mediation: A Guide for Mediators, Advocates, Advisers, Lawyers, and Students in Civil, Commercial, Business, Property, Workplace, and Employment Cases' by Jonathan Dingle with John Sephton
'The Mini-Pupillage Workbook' by David Boyle
'A Practical Guide to Crofting Law' by Brian Inkster
'A Practical Guide to Spousal Maintenance' by Liz Cowell
'A Practical Guide to the Law of Domain Names and Cybersquatting' by Andrew Clemson
'A Practical Guide to the Law of Gender Pay Gap Reporting' by Harini Iyengar
'A Practical Guide to the Rights of Grandparents in Children Proceedings' by Stuart Barlow
'NHS Whistleblowing and the Law' by Joseph England
'Employment Law and the Gig Economy' by Nigel Mackay & Annie Powell
'A Practical Guide to Noise Induced Hearing Loss (NIHL) Claims' by Andrew Mckie, Ian Skeate, Gareth McAloon
'An Introduction to Beauty Negligence Claims – A Practical Guide for the Personal Injury Practitioner' by Greg Almond
'Intercompany Agreements for Transfer Pricing Compliance' by Paul Sutton
'Zen and the Art of Mediation' by Martin Plowman
'A Practical Guide to the SRA Principles, Individual and Law Firm Codes of Conduct 2019 – What Every Law Firm Needs to Know' by Paul Bennett
'A Practical Guide to Adoption for Family Lawyers' by Graham Pegg
'A Practical Guide to Industrial Disease Claims' by Andrew Mckie & Ian Skeate
'A Practical Guide to Redundancy' by Philip Hyland
'A Practical Guide to Vicarious Liability' by Mariel Irvine
'A Practical Guide to Applications for Landlord's Consent and Variation of Leases' by Mark Shelton
'A Practical Guide to Relief from Sanctions Post-Mitchell and Denton' by Peter Causton
'A Practical Guide to Equity Release for Advisors' by Paul Sams
'A Practical Guide to Financial Services Claims' by Chris Hegarty

'The Law of Houses in Multiple Occupation: A Practical Guide to HMO Proceedings' by Julian Hunt
'Occupiers, Highways and Defective Premises Claims: A Practical Guide Post-Jackson – 2nd Edition' by Andrew Mckie
'A Practical Guide to Financial Ombudsman Service Claims' by Adam Temple & Robert Scrivenor
'A Practical Guide to Advising Schools on Employment Law' by Jonathan Holden
'A Practical Guide to Running Housing Disrepair and Cavity Wall Claims: 2nd Edition' by Andrew Mckie & Ian Skeate
'A Practical Guide to Holiday Sickness Claims – 2nd Edition' by Andrew Mckie & Ian Skeate
'Arguments and Tactics for Personal Injury and Clinical Negligence Claims' by Dorian Williams
'A Practical Guide to Drone Law' by Rufus Ballaster, Andrew Firman, Eleanor Clot
'A Practical Guide to Compliance for Personal Injury Firms Working With Claims Management Companies' by Paul Bennett
'RTA Allegations of Fraud in a Post-Jackson Era: The Handbook – 2nd Edition' by Andrew Mckie
'RTA Personal Injury Claims: A Practical Guide Post-Jackson' by Andrew Mckie
'On Experts: CPR35 for Lawyers and Experts' by David Boyle
'An Introduction to Personal Injury Law' by David Boyle
'A Practical Guide to Subtle Brain Injury Claims' by Pankaj Madan

These books and more are available to order online direct from the publisher at www.lawbriefpublishing.com, where you can also read free sample chapters. For any queries, contact us on 0844 587 2383 or mail@lawbriefpublishing.com.

Our books are also usually in stock at www.amazon.co.uk with free next day delivery for Prime members, and at good legal bookshops such as Wildy & Sons.

We are regularly launching new books in our series of practical day-to-day practitioners' guides. Visit our website and join our free newsletter to be kept informed and to receive special offers, free chapters, etc.

You can also follow us on Twitter at www.twitter.com/lawbriefpub.

www.ingramcontent.com/pod-product-compliance
Ingram Content Group UK Ltd.
Pitfield, Milton Keynes, MK11 3LW, UK
UKHW020150290926
15471UKWH00004B/794

9 781914 608322